CANDY
A Collection to Satisfy Your Sweetest Cravings

edited by
Dale Winslow and Erin Badough

NeoPoiesis Press, LLC

NeoPoiesis Press
P.O. Box 38037
Houston, Texas 77238-8037

www.neopoiesispress.com

Candy: a collection to satisfy your sweetest cravings
Copyright © 2009 by NeoPoiesis Press, LLC
Cover Design: Amanda Pierce
Introduction: Lance Strate
Interior Layout: Erin Badough
Individual Contributions Copyright © 2009 by their authors

All rights reserved. No part of this book may be used or reproduced in any manner whatsoever without express written permission from the publisher except in the case of brief quotations embodied in critical articles and reviews.

Candy: a collection to satisfy your sweetest cravings/ edited by Dale Winslow and Erin Badough
ISBN10 0-981-99840-4 (paperback : alk. paper)
      1. Erotic Poetry. I. Badough, Erin and Winslow, Dale

Printed in the United States of America.

First Edition

mulier cupido
quod dicit amanti,
in vento
et rapida scribere
oportet aqua.

-catullus-

Contents

introduction v

inhale
joed miller *1*

your ice wind
carol voccia *2*

creation
annette stenslien *3*

corner piece
bruce millar *4*

virgin lover
courtney ray *7*

girl loves girl love girl
samantha ledger *8*

desire
glenda shaw-garlock *9*

five small poems
bruce dorlova *10*

wrists bound high
t.k. ellington *11*

raw sex
shirley hall *12*

bubblepop
david arshawsky *13*

soulmate
curt murphy *15*

blue
jenny wear *17*

the virginal triptych
  josé e. del rosario *18*

the salty tango
  carol voccia *23*

safe harbor
  courtney ray *24*

white sound
  carol voccia *25*

after b'stilla, before the morning
  erin badough *27*

weight (wait) of tongue
  mary celeste nyberg *28*

grafenberg's anvil
  t.k. ellington *29*

cosmopolitan
  neil mccrea *32*

cloud
  david arshawsky *33*

horripilation
  samantha ledger *35*

chirography
  lance strate *36*

randomness
  amanda baker *37*

your pleasure
  nicole ficco *38*

mischa's conversation with the devil
  seb *39*

three breathing haiku
  bruce dorlova *40*

honeysuckle
annette stenslien... *41*

sensual scarification
dale winslow *42*

like molasses on a soft summer morning
erin badough.. *43*

learning to dodge bullets
neil mccrea.. *47*

blueberry pancakes
steve szewczok... *49*

midnight
melissa a. delise *51*

narcissistic lover
shirley hall *53*

it starts with a line
michelle warner *54*

doggystyle
nicole ficco.. *55*

origami
annette stenslien.. *56*

cantaor
anna donovan.. *57*

control
urban schrott... *58*

ginger crush
erin badough.. *59*

riding the shaman
dale winslow *61*

virgin four posted bed
joed miller.. *63*

exposed
michael farris 64

ising from the tarmac
carol voccia 65

accension
anna donovan 67

mother's milk
jason freiman 68

esurient
barbara w. mcgrory 69

lust can
michael farris 70

the lasting night of the lover
jonathon derrick wilson 71

in the worst way
t.k. ellington 73

bower
victoria fotios 74

drabbletini with a twist
barbara w. mcgrory 75

the kiss
nadine clayton 76

cinnamon kisses
glenda shaw-garlock 77

toetry
frank axworthy 79

kiss to crying
BlackMarket 80

insatiable night
courtney ray 81

maiden grass
anna donovan......83

there
barbara w. mcgrory......85

head sex
BlackMarket......86

the perfect canvas
brenda patricia garza......87

there is nothing better than sex in the kitchen
samantha ledger......89

this ancient song
bruce dorlova......91

oh yes
ross hamilton hill......92

felt
BlackMarket......93

augury
dale winslow......94

foreplay
josé e. del rosario......95

introduction

Painters and sculptors frequently turn to the human body as a subject, so that the nude is a commonplace in museums and art galleries. The artist's interest in the outer form of women and men as aesthetic, biological, and sexual beings is paralleled by the poet's concern with the body as topic, and as metaphor (some say the source of all metaphor). As we move from figure studies to figures of speech, we find the poet employing verbal description of the body, and its activities, both profound and profane, and perhaps more significantly, explorations of an interior landscape in which drives and desires, as well as passion and romance, play no small part. Sensual perception, musky memory, and sexual imagination all are vital parts of lived experience, a strange hybrid of that biological imperative that challenges self-control at every opportunity, and the higher mental and spiritual functions that elevate love, often beyond all other values and motivations, at times to the point of mystical experience. And this aspect of life is, therefore, a theme of great appeal for the poet, who seeks to answer the question, *what does it mean to be human?* To err is human, we are told, but it is no error to say that Eros is especially humanizing, hence the slogan from the sixties, *make love, not war!*

As a point of contrast, the art of the pornographer is a transparent one, both in the obvious aim of excitation and manipulation, but also in that the goal is to disguise the medium as much as possible, and generate the illusion of a direct and *immediate*, that is, *unmediated* experience. The art of erotic poetry is quite the opposite, as the poet's purpose is for readers and listeners to attend to the words themselves, to pay heed to the language, the sound, and the style that is employed, to find aesthetic pleasure in the composition in and of itself, an aesthetic pleasure that reflects, rather than just presents or represents the actual pleasure of human sexuality. In other words, the gratification offered by the *form* of erotic poetry mirrors the gratification we may gain from its *content*. And so, we may admire the craft that went into the making of the poem, perhaps even dissect the technique, or we may, at the other extreme, find ourselves in a Pygmalion-like state of arousal, or a Narcissus-like state of narcosis. But above all, the erotic mirror that these poets have fashioned allows us to examine ourselves, our needs and our wants, our experiences and intentions, our minds and our bodies, in all their beauty, and in their unattractive aspects as well. In short, the mirror of Eros allows us to *know* ourselves, in all of our humanity.

This collection is aptly named, for candy is sweet, but can sometimes cause us pain, in the form of a bellyache, and sometimes leave us empty, in regard to calories and cavities alike. *Candy* is also *candid*, having the virtue of honesty, providing forthright appraisals of individuals, relationships, and our species as a whole (and suggesting that "we must cultivate our garden," à la *Candide*). And most of all, *Candy* is a treat, one that has been lovingly crafted by our skilled confectioners, Erin Badough and Dale Winslow, who have put together this book *con* (that is, *with*) *affection*. As an edited collection, *Candy* is the product of collaboration, between the two editors, and among the thirty-seven poets included in this volume. Moreover, it is only fitting that this be the first work published by NeoPoiesis Press, itself a collaborative effort that I am pleased to be a part of, and a partnership that emerged out of the larger, looser collectivity that is the MySpace poetry community. This book is just the beginning of a series of publications that will feature a wide variety of styles, formats, topics and themes. It is just the beginning, and it is a very, very sweet beginning indeed!

Lance Strate, 2009

inhale

I want to taste the salty
peek of desire,
inhale the sweet,
musky smell of you,
tickle my skin on your fur.
Taste the full smoothness
that makes us whole,
lather and lace you
with kisses.
Tire my tongue and buzz
my lips,
Celebrate texture, pleasure,
pain, sensation.
Hear nothing but
the sound of your heartbeat
as the blood pulses through
your thighs.
Taste your heartbeat against
my teeth and tongue
and rock you until you
shudder from grief and pain,
triumph and pleasure
all at once and fall from grace
to breathlessly adore me.

joed miller

your ice wind

You consume me like ice wind
Etching me with your salt
Submitting
But aching to be in charge
My torched desire
Feasts like hot chilies
Sizzled red in my mouth
Turning you
Inside out
Gorging
Your guts
Blood letting droplets
Coat my chin and weep on my
Arms and legs
Your moon lips erotically
Exposed
Slapped until purpled
As you cry for me to never
Stop
Get on your knees
Wrap your heat around my
Fleshed thigh
Weep for my touch
I'll grant you everything your
Ice wind allows
I adore you gaping at my
Spice
While I crush you in my arms
And clamped embrace
Begging you to stay

carol voccia

creation

Kiss words
full mouthed
Lick slowly
their curiosity
Nibble the strands
of loose thought
tied not so neatly
Bring forth questions
hidden in comforts fold
Suck gradual
submission from each line
Embrace your sight

these visions, yours,
that bend the light
craft and create

This limitless capacity
yours, to place common
on a lazy susan
and boldly take it
in uncommon ways

Make those words come
by the tip of your pen
the stroke of your keys
Allow your voice range
uninhibited intimacy

with language,
multiples are your gift

annette stenslien

corner piece

She sits alone
in the corner,
without arms
to pull up
her knees
and hide

just in case
she gets cut
like the rest
of the cake;

I see her,
her top
so smooth
any knife
with a conscience
could do naught
but bow
to her,
as do I;

her sides
entice
my eyes
and cause me

 to draw straws
between
her moist filling
and her sugary skin;

her insides glisten
in anticipation
of my tongue;

her cream awaits
sweet release,

layered
deep within
her;

I hold her
gently
and she collapses
into me;

my tongue
applies
moisture
to her rose,

steady flicking
causes her
to shift slightly
as she feels
her cream
begin to rise;

her sides
splay wide as

I explore
her exquisite
tastes and textures

as pleasure builds

in her epicenter

 and soon
she loses
all cohesion,

she shakes
and convulses

as I fill her
with me
she fills me
with her

and I look back
to where I saw
a scared girl

and I see
a glow
brighter
than any candle;

she holds
my gaze
with
unspoken softness
clear as
unfettered dawn;

she is
no longer alone.

   bruce millar

virgin lover

Harness hangs her veil

Silk dressings tie hands
delicate bound in knot

Lips tulip
as his garden rose
waiting in the rouge of hue

Tears shower the rains
of desire to pluck
within the prick as bridle

undone, as anew

courtney ray

girl loves girl love girl

undertones of flesh
catch hot beneath these sheets
of love, that bow and rise
to the melody of our hearts,
capture my breath;
I am restless in my longing -
a lusting for your lips,

curling hips that lift or drift
towards the unfurling petals
of your sweet umber,
to slumber I - in waves
of coiling ecstasy.
Humming bird - I quiver
at your touch,

to linger in the furrows
of fields of skin,
that spread content
across this white expanse,
to sleep my love -
to dream
of waking in dawn's cool morning
and begin again anew,
this simple love
burning with passionate hunger.

samantha ledger

desire

Come close to me,
I am your beguiling Salome
Scented tresses and honey skin
Let me lay you down
Supine between my thighs
Allow me to trace your contours
With my tongue
Let me worship your body
With burnt saccharine lips
And undulating hips
My longing now fully unveiled
Does my artful flesh delight?
Does your racing heart take flight?
As my breath paints your bare skin...

glenda shaw-garlock

five small poems

just there
your scent
i am undone
.

speak to me
use
only vowels
.

your steady gaze
thick in the

space

between us
.

the back of my hand
grazes
your lips flower

.

this
thick
tongue
treacle

x

bruce dorlova

wrists bound high

Wrists bound high,
a candle at my feet,
a single salted finger to sup,
to shush me to disjointed silence.
A ragged nail
dragged deliberate across slacked lips
teasing out the pinkish fish.
Her panting gills flit full
with salivary jewels
delight.
A silver tipped baton
cold and hard against jostled loins
commands
and I obey.
Slow stroked dalliance,
a moon glared tryst
tantrum interplay
sprayed of tantric spark.
Rush,
my head fills
encircled of loomed cloud
lathered of the dark
that shelters my flesh.
It slides quicksilver down the neck,
races swift to the nipped tips
areola bloomed bliss-
leaps jubilant to martyrs death.
It lays
this liquid leather black
tongue flat against my navel,
slides knowing between thighs
that for her sweetest tortures ache.

t.k. ellington

raw sex

womanhood overwhelms me
wetness rushing glands
waves of arousal boiling blood
inflame my yin
my yang

passion's breathing pinnacles
plateaus a hymen's tear
shades of rose bejewels my thighs
beguile my yin
my yang

a pubic arch ascending
a clitoris unconstrained
erectile tissues fill with blood
induce my yin
my yang

raw sex overwhelms me
locked in this infamous game
a vaginal fornix enraptures
enthralling my yin
my yang

your roving tongue provokes me
excites my clitoral head
waves of euphoria engage my yin
eruptions
still my yang

shirley hall

bubblepop

so what, the paper won't come off
now that the lazy red candy paints your tongue
and sticky sweet in this summer moment
i can't look away
red, like your candy lips
that luxurious tongue, that innocent lick
and your candy nails
and your honeyed eyes
as you crack the skin
to bite the pink pliant center
and twist out the stick
crushing the tart shards of red into the gum
releasing great and joyous pleasure
it is I, between your molars
only to break my bubble
with a snap and a stare

david arshawsky

soulmate

Tha mornin air
 is crisp and clean.
Dew drops in summer
spill cool upon my feet
and I think of you.
Those slow subtle kisses.
Tha softness of your throat
warm, pressin flesh
and tha sounds of your
pleasure

I am captured, sweet Lady
truly captured...

Your vision is nectar
that nourishes my soul
and draws my heart
out of shelters
long built,
rarely forsaken.
Tha taste of you lingers
upon my lips and I
fear its departure.
For I have not felt
such deep caress
in tha center of
my spirit before
being graced
by your
fragrance...

You are my goddess.
I lay naked before you

for God himself
fused your glory

and touched
my soul with tha
essence of
your presence...

curt murphy

blue

Consuming sultry hot liquid
her skin grows damp for you,
as under dark summer skies
your tongue traces
a silvery path
across her flesh,
mapping the dips and curves.

You whisper
naughty nothings,
nip at tender lobes,
scratching desires
rake across her flesh
as she shakes
uncontrollable need.

In the dusky light
she feels the shadows
of the face,
swallows your gaze
and watches the passion spread.

Taking you in complete,
she opens up,
allowing the heat to rise
in familiar blushes.

Afterwards she's
all consumed,
lovely
yet secret,
a sister of forgotten
summer mornings.

Her skin bruised,
tongue dry,

after your songs so blue,
she leaves.

jenny wear

the virginal triptych

anaxarete

At first you were just an illusion;
pyrite of flesh and desires.
You were so tantalizing,
flirting with yourself at the bar.
Standing monumentally
within all your glory and morbid delight.
You played with your hair,
weaving your fingers into lockets of lust.

A bete noire dressed in attraction;
you were so mesmerizing,
so idyllic and phantom like.

Making silent promises
with every napkin fold.
Every action, reaction,
fusion
of alcohol and mischievousness.

An all and out elusive game of Go
Against all of us,
wavering and resisting,
black and white;
revolution and fascination
of longing, giving and taking.

With your wet lips,
you toyed with the rim of that poor glass.
You slithered into angular motions
of bitter seduction and syrupy vertigo.

Your eyes were ours to hold for a
second
as your numbing smile slipped
in and out of our attention.

Never faltered, never there.
Forever captivating, forever here.

We committed suicide in pirouettes
of flamboyancy and desperation.
Like silly silicon peacocks we strut
our sleight of hand and distractions.
We side step and waltz,
we vanish and fall.
Our fancy crushed by the lessening
gravel that your addictive curves dropped.

When the song stopped
you left us all at the dance floor,
perishing away in latent pulses
of smoke and lights.
You walked out the door
to what they guess was a
perpetual
sleep of granite and marble.

In the end,
you were just
brimstones and crystals;
an illusion and a sculpture
of fire and ice.
We were just
a die and a roll upon your grainy fingers.

Forever lust.

Forever stone.

and the night whispered a zephyr

There was no beginning,
we found each other in the interlude of the evening.
Between burning incenses
my desires followed your stretched hands.

(Like a vessel upon a starry sky)
Everything else was insubstantial;
encapsulated by the echoes of our clash,
not a sigh was trivial,
for us
we were the world beneath our covers.
Derived from ardor,
integrating every known formulation.
dynamics and heat;
a fulminating system of veiled lovers.
The night whispered a zephyr of lust
and we additively inhaled synergy.

Conjuring real miracles
amidst pulsations and boundless positions.
We rediscovered every edge,
curve, finesse, subtlety and perverted delicacy.
Chemistries and outbursts;
indulging a distorted calyx of flesh,
sweat and liquid dreams
that began and had a delta in your mouth and my feet.
It wasn't satiating, it was squandering,
it was burning and forever burning into fantasies;
ellipsis of animal savagery
and carnal sagacity in spurts of aphonia.
The night whispered a zephyr of lust
while we delightedly dissipated in synergy.

We whispered a zephyr to our own image,
like the night that dilapidated under our lust.
We made out of our frenzy and our moans
a beginning in the synthesis of our synergy.
We parted from a partition of selfishness;
from conquests, nibbles, longing, scratches
and the burning chaos to the virtues parted,
the conjoint secrets and the lust that made us whole.
From a deluge of desires and bounds
we forged creation, we were mortal gods.
From your submissive genuflection upon me,
to an impartial inflection of joy and love.

And the night whispered a zephyr of lust
and we just heard love upon the fresh lips of our synergy.

valles marineris

If men are from Mars, why are you the Genesis?

The night labyrinth
embraces your heart;
an isthmus of yearning and ill-fancy
tangled between chaos and passion.

And you sway amongst us,
you glide with your cloth of lust.

With a subtle kiss it all began,
you suppressed and oppressed without time.
you forged my desires under your skin,
to just then ever orbit in maddening silence.

And you sway amongst us,
you caress our countenance with your sins.

In an anti-matter of moments and fractions
you enslaved and tossed me away.
You were my satellite of sensations,
I was the halo of dust and gas that you absorbed.

And you sway amongst us,
with Venus as your talisman of alchemy.

There's an abyss in your soul;
a valley of superfluous moons.
The scarlet of your wickedness
gave birth to your violent irises.

And you sway amongst us,
spiral of seduction and malice.

The helix, double and inverse
it is just but a myth.
Beneath your warm and tender lips
lies the mouth of the universe
infinite.

josé e. del rosario

the salty tango

Silk straining beneath heavy hands
Punctuating nipples
Press hip to molten pelvic
Rotating bellies

A convex concave tango

Pull my mouth into your sucking breath
Ride my tongue with liquid
Lips and salivating kisses
Cut to your knees
Find my salty delta
A thick forest of musk

Breathe your fire in seams of pink
Shiver ridges of flaming thick flesh
You ride deep
The jellied moon
Coming to the howling dog

carol voccia

safe harbor

Mesmerize floating
as one repeat
to dock

Lily skin
mountains soft to ply
hard chrisom

Cherry blossoms in
lips so tender
to picnic

Moonlit silken tides
in safe harbor radiate
rhythm, storming

As eyes close, within the ache
throttle so slow

Tongues trace sonnets
hungry, fingers eager
explore-open

And my mouth travels down
deep the hours into endless…

Succumbing a taunt
begging in the diligent-must
of promises, to keep
suckling sweet the ripple

Into one heart-quench
starving to feed another
in fantasies-infinite.

courtney ray

white sound

You leave succulent poems on my pillows
As you cover your face screaming inside them
With ecstasy from my potent love
I scoop you from the fragments
Of cotton and sage
Pressing your wild lips
Into dangling adjectives
My heart pounds out
Rivers of cream and
Twisted joy
Scribing you inside my iris
I have fallen inside your vessel of
Golden straw
Let me write in your veins
Leaving my nail scratches and
Scribbling
And all that is you I adore
I'll paint the sides of buildings
With your steam
You scream poems into my pillow
Writhing in gasps
As I lick your ass finding the root
And I tangle your deaf white sound
On the tip of my pen

carol voccia

after b'stilla, before the morning

Her hair, infused,
with chai, spice
of hot tea and
honey drops

saffron threaded
'round the bare
of her neck

and the sweat from
heat of night
dripped
dissolved
the delicacy
'til drizzling
down her chest
infusing her skin
with desert marinade

and the drums played
louder
the smoke of bubbled meat
mixing with torching flame
fugitive temptation
from the heavy tajine
buried below

and he placed the remains
of the charmoula upon her stomach
and devoured the meal
as slowly as permitted
drinking her sex from her navel
rising in the fall of rapid breath

and the shadows danced
along her length
feisty fairies waving feathered fronds
in the sea-flung wind

and the feast
from the coal-glow
dissolved into shreds of lamb
upon her heated tongue
teasingly falling from his
roughened fingers

only softened by the
pumice of her curves
the dark curls
falling over dark eyes
hiding the blush from view

rising from a wandering
caress

and a whispered hush

erin badough

weight (wait) of tongue

my stomach dishes
clustered calico
red curtained toilet
jerk, jerk silent
my cool voice, my loud desire
o sister you are plume
chiseled with tongue
twisted on flowered sheets
tingle and surge between legs
rocking to Admiral Halsey
under our canopy at midnight

mary celeste nyberg

grafenberg's anvil

I
measured of callous thrust
lightning deep
between spread lips

I
Thor
rampage
hammering sparks
off anvil dark
spit bloodied from grinding Ragnarok's
fluvial

You
leak cumulus succubus screams
from crevasse
riotous tectonic shifts
 I am catgut
cut swage over finger plucked
dreamed out vibrations raised
from inner strings

I
am tracker seer hunter
wild abandon
and am devoured of you
squeezed between Gibraltar and Styx
you tumble down over me
in violent folds of flesh
boned sinewy frenzy
bury me in mottled earth
and tumbled aggregate

your skin liquid
melts steel
whets to mercurial dust.

      t.k. ellington

cosmopolitan

Earth goddess in youth
breasts of paleolithic fantasy,
flat stomach and wide hips.
Sex with her was languorous and warm,
blanket wrapped and adrift
on a warm watered ocean,
but there were waves.

We met on set.
A student film, solidly sci-fi.
I played a barfly and would be rapist,
comically cast without need to audition.
She ran sound,
held boom mikes, rolled tape,
and kept quiet on the set.

Some positions perplexed her
and condoms confused.
Face planted in pillow,
her posterior presented,
she would constantly chatter,
"like this, or like that?"
Riding on top
she'd slide suddenly sideways
and I'd have to remind her
that boners don't bend.
Perusing the prophylactic
she would question
its size, shape and substance.

The rape scene ran everyone ragged
jokes and jests were rampant
and kept the actors sane.

During a long set up
I confided in the sound op,
I'd had sex, sure, but never a girlfriend,

I freakishly found sex and friendship
completely incompatible.
After a long day, she suggested a date.
I smiled and shrugged,
"Only for sex."
She said that would be swell.

As I descended toward her center
she held my head
and told me I didn't need to.
" . . . but what if I want to?"
There was no reply as I began
to nuzzle and nibble, lick and lap.
Her hands flew spastic
not knowing where to rest,
her legs rose once then lay limp
until she savagely bumped and bucked.
She shouted, "What the hell just happened?"

One rainy weekend, months later,
I arrived home and my ragged roomie
slurped his ramen and mumbled,
"Some ratfaced girl was looking for you."
I had no clue and little curiosity
as to who this had been,
until he retrieved a familiar phone number.

His insult towards her made me wax weird.
I could see why he said it,
but it couldn't have occurred to me on my own.
I realized that maybe I'd missed more.
Mentally surveying our sex scene,
I felt that if I wasn't her first
I was certainly close.
With her beauty slighted
and her inexperience made plain
I puffed up protective
and padded off to her place.

Comely in a kimono, she welcomed me warmly.
She sat me down sweetly,
and proceeded to praise me.
"Your cosmopolitan attitude has given me courage."
I laughed at the description,
but she pressed on.
She now dated regularly,
where she hadn't before.
She had called up to tell me
what a good deed I'd done.
I blushed and I stammered,
then laughed when I said,
"I'd be glad to do good
if that's all it took!"

neil mccrea

cloud

i remember your skin as i pulled you in from the rain
from your mouth, hot breath like cloud,
hair pulled back, it was all your mouth could do
drank rain from soft curves
blood pressed as wet hands pull me away
sank low into you, under you, our tongues spoke truth for once
in knowing, left nothing for show, for pose, just clouding breath

out of minds, out of clothes

david arshawsky

horripilation

Under sheet of red velvet
run long stemmed fingers.

Come.

Sigh.

Breathe.

May I meet you half way;
between dusk and dark
to embark upon journeys
to valleys deep and wide.

Such roads spread far
beyond the reach of moral men -
gallant knights have rested
wretched at the wayside;
forgotten dreams lingering on their lips.

These hips turning
urging on the reaches of your touch.
Tender words that brush
smooth against my cheek.

How I seek you out.

All shallow doubt drifts;
melodious moments of heart beats.
Solidarity stands against no woman

I am your voice
as you are mine.

Between time
we greet with kisses
full and red,
cradle places of wondered lust;

thrust forward with hunger
until I slumber in the crook
of your muscled arm.

Charming you;
watching my eyes
flutter closed to dreamscapes.

Holding hair and tears in your hands
deep days and long nights
under starlight burning day back.

Fearful of the dawn,
graceless I gather you;
in hands and mouths and meaning
seemingly seeing eternal
the youth of love
in its age old ageless entirety.

samantha ledger

chirography

The old man in the scriptorium
sat at his carrel and copied
the ancient manuscript,
dried and brittle with age,
letter by letter,
word by word,
sentences resounding over centuries,
handwritten memories coming to mind,
dreaming, as he wrote...

>   I dip my pen
>   into your inkwell
>   and sign my name
>   in strokes long, hard, and bold.
>   My goose quill quivers
>   as I leave my mark
>   on your soft, smooth vellum.
>   I am your scribe.
>   My calligraphy illuminates
>   your tightly bound codex,
>   a colophonic ending
>   to another session of copying,
>   reproduction without replication,
>   a ritual repeated with variation.
>   Puritanical types call it corruption,
>   not recognizing a labor of love,
>   a carnal craft,
>   the most intimate of encounters,
>   two minds becoming one,
>   thoughts tracing patterns for the eye to see,
>   words working into flesh,
>   worlds waiting to be reborn...

The old man smiled,
and snored...

>   *lance strate*

randomness

I need poetry today,
sex and wild onions beneath
the precise blue of
breathless summer skies,
and death.

I need cold potato soup,
skinned knees and coffee
with a stranger's hand
up my denim skirt,
and beauty.

I need bruised apples,
dirty laundry and the
symphony of a million
stars gently dying,
and you.

amanda baker

your pleasure

Find myself falling into the lust in your eyes
Taste the sin melting between my thighs
Pure honey rain remains tracing wet paths
Beneath my body, warm from the touch of your mind
Synaptic caress sending little tingles down the arch of my back
Mind stuck in a labyrinth made from an ecstasy pose
Walls made from your flesh twisted in a silent moan
My stare traces your lines, sweet contours begging
To be licked slowly with the tip of a pink tongue
All roads lead to a taste of heaven, sugar melting into salt
Path laid in kisses down a trail made of a smile
My fingers walk their own road without a thought
The world dissolves outside of this stroke
Single tip pressed tightly to the button that lets me feel
The intricate sketched flip book sliding across my grey matter
Swallowed by an intent gaze into your rapture
Seconds turn to minutes, minutes turn to hours
Hands soaked to bone…marrow weeping tears of bliss
I find myself falling back against the pillows
Spent from swimming in the lust in your eyes
Wading in the honey rain between my thighs
I find myself in the sated in your pleasure

nicole ficco

mischa's conversation with the devil

"Get behind me Satan"
Mischa said with firm conviction.
So Satan lifted his head from her shoulder
and slid 'round to the rear
He stroked the smooth lines
from her hips to her thighs
and gasped as he saw the
graceful curve of her spine.
He stretched his fingers
to that certain spot
and Mischa's neck arched
as she laid her head back
and closed her eyes
and murmured "Devil, Devil, Devil
just this once…"

    seb

three breathing haiku

breathe your life into my o-
these pained and jagged
lungs i gasp my eyes fly wide

-oOo-

this resonation of hearts
these blind vibrations
we are open to the sky

-oOo-

my lips move when i read you
breathing deep and quick
flesh rises up to meet me

bruce dorlova

honeysuckle

Beautiful as the sun
pull flower
from stem
place in your mouth

nature's juice will come
perfect and pure
as honey
on your tongue

annette stenslien

sensual scarification

your quick, paper cut
    kisses
pattern me; trails ripe
    red
tongue whipped; willingly
    tied
by these bindings that will not
    break.
raw response to blistering
    caress.
flesh to marrow
    undressing
my skin to yours
    sewing
sinew to sweat
    sharing
sutured regrets
    dissolving
the scars of our uncertain
    success.

I am sustained by this;

your iron
        lung

our lingering
        kiss…

    dale winslow

like molasses on a soft summer morning

unbuckle straps of shoes binding ankles
unhook garters from your skin, clipped black
roll the stockings down, over scarred knees
palmed lightly as thumbs travel up thighs
to cheeky lace
slipping down, silken,

your breath fogging, staggered,
as fingers trace nuclear orbits around navel
and wrap around waist, seeking the hooks
binding your breasts,
wires underneath falling free as lips graze

your graceful form, curls kissing your neck,
tightened throat,
teeth punctuating your ripening
until tongue teases in echoing rhythm

rock and sway upon upbeats
of a slow Spanish song
violin singing on a high pitch string

tauter than the tight grasp of wet brown hair
under your knuckles
you rise as the tempo slides along faster

when the bow
                               snaps
and you collapse
breathless
eyes closed

heart pounding through the arteries
trembling in your open legs.

a complete permutation

       erin badough

learning to dodge bullets

I.

She caught me skulking beside the bookstore,
another sad sack scoping her out.
The book selling babe
was a Mensa member
with callipygian curves,
she seemed certain
to shoot me down
and mock my awkward gawking.
Before I could begin badinage,
she cradled my crotch
while quietly
inviting me to coffee.

We quaffed caffeine,
cozy on couches.
The subject of sex slid sideways
and careened off the corners
of our conversation.
Something sparked
when I spoke of sex as
transformative and transcendent,
and she declared,
if pregnancy, disease, and social stigma
could be avoided

she would make it her mission
to fuck everyone in the world.

I sat in silent surprise,
as she spun scenarios:
She prophesied a new pedagogy for pubescents
as she loosed lessons in fellatio upon them.
An anarchic angel among ancients
she wanted to recreate the raunchiest
memories of the elderly
and promise new pleasures to old flesh.

She dreamed of dangerous dalliances
with every amateur Adonis and veritable Venus,
to bathe in their beauty
while they wallowed in her worship.
She'd slowly strip for the deaf
and sing her orgasms to the blind.
She wished to experience every ecstasy
of the facile and friendless
and knew they'd be better off for it.

At my quiet query
she tut tutted all taboos
and sought sex with family too.
She craved caresses
from hands that had held
her infant body
and sought sexual congress
with the source of her existence,
both seminal spark
and withered womb.
I accepted the napkin
with her number on it,
even as I struggled
with the image of her head
upon her Mee Maw's lap.

II.

Days went by,
and I didn't dial.
Those digits daunted me,

was I terribly turned on
or trepidatious
over an id unleashed?

When passing the post office
traffic tried to entangle me,

and a back road detour
seemed a solid solution.
Bare skin in a backyard
forced my foot to the brakes.
Vic Hugo noted,
"a naked woman is a woman armed, "
and this sun bathing siren
held a howitzer.
It was the troubling book babe
making Miss Mansfield
look like a lackluster
Olive Oyl.
I transformed into a Tex Avery wolf
and was soon saturated in my own salivation.
Fearful of my potential for foolishness,
I flew home,
but now I nursed a heavy hunger.

Memory fades,
but the digits must have been dialed
and a date was made.
We rolled retro rock-a-billy
and bounced beautifully
into a bowling alley
filled with tiresome teens
too young yet
to meet and mate
in clubs and bars.

We giggled at our own glamour,
debauched gods in a nine lane Olympus.

Although pleased
that this oddball date
had gone pitch perfect,
my soul sickened
as she assured me
her caffeine crazed
sexual soliloquy
was entirely serious.

No psychic, I nonetheless
saw a firm future before me,
filled with drug drama,
jealousy jags,
and arbitrary accusations.
I'd perpetually pursued
bad girls and wicked women,
as a sailor I'd lost many a ship
to a song,
but that night I discovered I need not
and I plugged my ears to the sound.
There was a kiss and a cuddle,
followed by lingering lust
but I went home alone
secure in my new ability
to dodge bullets.

neil mccrea

blueberry pancakes

Eggs mix with the milk
of my pancake thoughts,
flowered scent of bacon
flavors the kitchen air.

Raw is how you feel in this bowl
as I whisk you to your completeness.

The pan is hot
enough to cook you
without the burning.

That's how much I love you.

As I pour you out
I watch you sit there
in your batter blue.

The berry of you begins
it's weeping

seeping your berry blood
in the sweetness of my batter

anywhere
but in between promises.

Everything
that love is worth mixes

within this batter

past the shadows
that fall down whenever we meet.
I am fractured by the spell your cooking puts me in.

Magic pan blows his flute.

In this bubbled batter bliss,
the blueberries
surrender to their cooking.

You are free now,
out from the pan
and into my mouth
wherein
I can taste you whole.

In the brilliance told here on my plate,
my breakfast lies

in the accomplishment of you!

steve szewczok

midnight

Midnight:
the evening is young...

As she lay there sleeping,
the arch of her back beckons me.
My fingers dance,
down
the nape of her neck
down
the small indent of spine.

Her body is nothing less,
than magnificent.

She awakens…
She turns…
She smiles…

As she lay there breathing,
I study the landscape before me.
My palm dances,
down
the curve of her chin
down
the structure of shoulder.

In the warmth of her bosom,
I find solace.

She lifts…
She turns…
She sways…

As she lay there moaning,
I tangle my fist in her hair.
My mouth dances,
down
the sweat on her stomach

down
the line of her hip.

My nose pressed firm,
I obsess over her smell.

She shakes…
She turns…
She screams…

As she lay there in bliss,
I whisper "I've only just begun".
My body slides
down
down
down
to kiss her lips.

Twilight:
the day has just begun…

I am but a woman trained for survival
and better than he ever will be!

    melissa a. delise

narcissistic lover

Excuse me
may I break your rules
and touch you
I want to feel our fingers
inter-twined
your taboos of confiding lust
are lucid
may I place your hands
between my sultry thighs

apologies for unnerving
whilst you're resting
this emptiness consumes
my every thought
will you touch me if I promise
not to bate you
I recognize the keen of
your disgust
forgive annoying flaunts
of warmth and passions
I wear them in the sadness
of my eyes
my wedding vows preclude
adulterous pleasures
these reins of marriage vest
my deafening cries

excuse me
may I break your rule
and stroke you
my stretched libido seeds
an odious thatch

my riotous passions crave
clitoral pleasures

at times a woman needs
a human touch

shirley hall

it starts with a line

running smooth like the
side of his thumb against

the line of her belly
of her bottom lip

against the eye
the side of her thigh

the eye lid
the knuckle
 the belt buckle

the sigh and moan
of flight

to the same place
at the same time

for the same
capsulated mid night

swallowed like a
necessary fight

running tight like
the sigh of his engine

against the size of
her tide

it starts with a line

michelle warner

doggystyle

Back to basics a call to nature's wild
Collar on this animal not ready to be unleashed
Whimpers softly begging for a bone
Wag it in front of me, little tastes across my lips
To watch me drool and beg for you
Big puppy dog eyes look up pleading with you
To pet me, rub me, scratch all the right places
Get behind me and command me to cum
Make me pant your name off my tongue
Spank me for my refusal to roll over
I want to stay on all fours…until you can no longer
Hold my leash…and I am released
To mount you and bury my favorite bone.

nicole ficco

origami

Unique, I become
more than,
In your hands
I rise
soft friction
upon warm palms
knowing fingers

my form folds
over under
curved I become

a wing-spread swan
a blossoming lotus

open full
I fly

    annette stenslien

cantaor

He sings in cello voice
dark as bruises,
sharpened ironies
with counter-melodies
fluid in gestures,
mélange cascades
sift sun and shadow,
ancient spirits pass
behind his eyes,
and in passion trance
vanish into flame,
wind and moonlight glints
dense with quince trees.

His eyes burn,
amber consonance of sullen ways,
moody as Moorish facades,
frame of dark hair
whose ringlets follow
their own directive
and trail as they will
down a sinuous, strong back.

He is languid lust,
sweet spot linger,
paradox of causality,
jagged base notes,
spellbound love,
the verge of involuntary,
double jointed growls.

anna donovan

control

You know
That you are expected
To look strictly your best
And that your opinion on the matter
Shall not be taken into consideration

You know
That you are expected
To always be tasteful
And never vulgar in appearance
As it is distracting and redundant

You know
That you are expected
To make certain my pleasure
And only draw yours from sensing
You have not been found wanting

But you also know
That you are expected
Like ice on whipped flesh
For the tormenting promise of your scent
Awakens demons and unbinds desires

And you know
That you are expected
With unbearable anticipation
And that it is not a question of control
But unquestionable and uncontrollable

Yes, you know
That you are expected
To play your part well
So that you receive whatever is everything
If I also play mine

urban schrott

ginger crush

When you lick the plump of your lips,
I can tell you want to taste me;
that slow, salacious stalking
as you slant into my reach.

I savor saliva from your mouth
as you taunt my tongue with yours,
running smooth hands along my arms,
touch tingling soft on spine.

Tease, I whisper in your ear,
gruff and husked with longing.
You kiss me silent, suckle sweet,
and linger, loosely, guiling.

Reaching hungry 'neath my blouse
you love me lewdly, nip to teeth.
I shudder, ache, with scalding want,
fingers comb your curls, approving.

Between taut, strictured legs I reach
find your heat brimming, ready.
Two fingers reach in depth at first
'til slender fist fills liquid space.

I claim you mine, work meticulous
my darling, as we rock, breast to breast.
And you ease your savagery upon my skin
as I drive you to the brink of bliss

And you tumble over, crumpled, on my chest.

Eyes closed, you catch your breath,
and I feel you wander to my downy depths,
nails prickling along the journey.

erin badough

riding the shaman

kiss
  of scales set close
  to forked flicker
  slide of curve convex
  concave
  this undulating want
  slip of serpent dance cross
  supine white
  rough familiar touch
  of snake to sand
  sidewinder kiss
  rigid lick of heated tongue
  darting
  dance of shaman
  thrust
  fire circles
  leap
  deep swing of curved sweet
  glide of tongue
  to whispered breath
  quick plunge of tasting
  pull of aching wet
  grip and sway
  hard length of hot
  pulse
  strain of urgent
  stroking
  tight rise of fire
  spine undone
  tracing tips cross swelling
  shudder
  sharp exhales meet
  meld
  inhales joined
  tight slide of serpent
  dance
  fervent fingers in
  dampened dew

lips to heat
bloom of weeping nectar to skin
salted curve edged
by glide of tongue
lingering taste
of white heated
swells

    dale winslow

virgin four posted bed

four legged posted
each sweet soft cheek
placed upon four pillow high,
clouds touching
tempered between
valley yet unseen,
trimmed soft clean.
satin lash to bind
bed leg to yours,
wrists as well,
passions swell,
scents hidden within
now perfume the air
with lines perfection
from toe to nape of neck
a rolling seaside trail of tongues pleasures
treasured...
like christmas eve new toys surround
no finger to touch all ten securely bound.
am i...
... are you
whose face subdued??
jungle beats fill the space
and to feet's bottoms
first taste of moist lips
lightly placed...
but once then twice,
legs spread wide as guides
each soft globe whipped gently red,
then kissed wet
till valley blooms...
hand wrapped as sheath
it strokes beneath...
hot breath sweating upon your lowest back,
tightened fingers surround,
prickly fire upon flowered head
hills found beneath each palm...
now spread,

all treasures within clearly shown…
gifts to the senses,
visions of taste
shapes quickly growing…
each now free from the shadows
ready for open mouth to feed...
suckled whole and within
each slip of tongue..
.. of lip
is heard...
unable to move,
except from within
boundless rivers burst forth...
sweet loves fresh froth…
shoulder licked,
tilted head ear bitten
what once was forbidden
now in quick gasps
taken deeply,
thrilled,
white filled,
lava hot...
all given...
in moans and sighs
unfelt before
now
forgiven...

joed miller

exposed

I smell the texture of her skin
hear the weight of her voice
the slight movement
her body makes
as it slants toward the warmth.

A touch sings gentle
then intense
approaching her waist.

The lips close and then open
breathing in the last point
of restraint.

Red heat and then white
separate then liquid
flowing then cooled
reformed then settled
into a different space.

An elegant dance
wrapped in shyness
blanketed by mystery
raw as exposed life.

michael farris

rising from the tarmac

Rolling through velvet steam
wet dips my aching tongue to your
wild electric
charged with your scent and
comly melting flood
cascading down mouth and chin
rising up to meet again the
coaxing tip of my tongue lashing
deeper still against your hidden powerhouse
of potant thrust
find the highway and lift your wheels
separating tarmack peals away
and you soar
all stopps pulled as you ride the thick
air of cream rising into ether
and I ride with you
as passenger
and pilot
of your rushing journey
into waves of stars and molten bellies

carol voccia

accension

An inner nod confirms
the command to dance,
and veils follow
the elusive
shapeshifting allure
of ripe womanhood.

Finger cymbals
mingle melody and rhythm,
in restless conversing
of wind and flame.

Tussles of supple midriff muscles,
promise of flailing flesh
and passion contouring
the cyma curves of legs.

Hips in a
lazy Cabriolet of beadwork
whirling as night
through bare branches,
glimpse of nomad eyes,
a smolder of light
through cubical houses,
solemn and pale
under the weight
of Allah's hand.

Tease of a veil's edge
in the corner of a
musk stone rosebud mouth,
ache of sand to be traced
with serpentine ways.

There, over the horizon's line,
over muezzin morning murmurs,
Berber birds in the brush,
muffled baked earth,

stir of weaving looms,
entangled claims of kingdoms
and crowns.

She is the act of kindling,
sway of Infinity signs
over the center axis of mankind,
the flicker of recognition in my eyes,
the reason why men reach with tall towers,
wage war with the yearning to devour,
while confounded back to the babble
they were born speaking.

       anna donovan

mother's milk

positioned fetally for a taste
of lapped luxury
denied for vanity's sake
this tongue wondered
coaxing lips to suckle
buds cooing, wailing
like the babe before them

hungry hands grappled
repelling this happy trail
to the snug, damp cavern below

surrendered
smooth scene surveyed
lovers' argot allowed
lavish lingo
tantalizing tips and lips
swollen in anticipation
expectancy and...

wondrously honeyed hole
fished
so deliciously
patiently
deliberately 'til
mountains quaked
shaking rivers, sweat
from brows, backs
arched in amorous

gleaming teaming
droplets of delightful dew
dripped dotting lips and tips
kissed for many returns
to mother's milk

jason freiman

esurient

my culinary libido could not only devour you,
...then,
I have to talk about you; think about you
                        obsess over you
as

(bien cuit...)
         an exquisite taste;
a perfect morsel on my tongue...

(and the esthetic scintillation of elemental dancing across opulent wares...)

                                      (oh...)
  to come;
     to realize the lust
involved
the tender preparation
of desire to feed me;
abundant with earthy aromas,
teased; to the tooth
my excited hesitation into deviant experimentation
   lures me
        beyond
                  satiation
where delicious mistakes can be just as much fun...
esculent, I melt into your decadent gallantry
                      at once and finally
understanding

the meaning of hunger

    barbara w. mcgrory

lust can

An imagined fire
heating like the sun
borrowing the soul;
sweating with touch,
coveting the heat
instead of the warmth.

Lingering
beneath the surface
with satin possibilities;
hidden expectations
waiting like a match
for a surface strike
not knowing if
it will ignite a flame.

Hands leaving a trace
of want,
a smell of pepper
sensing the naked skin.

This pull caresses
a moment's sigh;
an imagined grind,
a seeking ache,
a moist breathing
in refrain.

She opens her eyes
to close them again.

He joins the feast.

michael farris

the lasting night of the lover

the slide of her skin,
popsicle melting-
slow
slowly;
draining the sun-God
from my strength

strong, the wind
on the nape of her neck
lick-lapping
double purring

9 lives too few for the kitty

moans
slave
the screams

in glass,
the kept are hidden
locked away to peak

i peaked;

down
she slides

sliding

in wars
i'll sleep and smile
in her, as i drink the moon drops
and share my fever.

jonathon derrick wilson

in the worst way

Yeah,
she wants me
in the worst kind of way,
whips (with and without Cream)
satin covered chains
leather bindings
little electro stimulators
innocuously placed,
you know what I mean…
She wants me
in the 'Worst' kind of way.

Little telepathic reminders in a crowded room
say that we're the only two
who are really there.
Yeah,
that kind of way.

I found that
eavesdroppings hit the flow
with a damnable splash
and make an abominable mess.

But in this reticular smelting of
booze infused Muses,
it would be hard not to catch a blurb
or high, floated though
caught at random,
from among the roaring in the lion's din.

 She asked if we were together,
casually floated
(a sinking feeling in my stomach)
I knew she was probing
(like a nearsighted hung-over proctologist
with numbness in the fingertips).

She was told
that the young lady with me
wasn't my wife,
but one of several (suck-retaries)
receptionists
from the (orifice)
office.
I
a professional lush
(and part-time accountant)
was well into my fifth Whiskey Sour,
as evidenced by the
(walking of a tightrope) way
I had of
(staggering as I was double-crossing)
entering a room.

      t.k. ellington

bower

Obscenely petalled bulbousity.
Surging explosion of sex.
Scent of heavy water drips
With pungent fermentation
To pull in and grip hold.

Intoxicated air.
Oxygen overtaken
By compressed fragrant stench.
Heady temptation
Holds the face,
Drags it down.
Submit,
Drink.

Stretched prone across the arched ribs,
Rattlesnake hooks secure its
Dangle of ripened luxury,
Brushing the brow with temptation.

Try to pass.
Parry the urge
To cup and penetrate.

Abandon the senses,
Scoop and slurp in
The Rose,
By another Name,
Darkly sweet.

victoria fotios

drabbletini with a twist

dirty, shaken, pimento-stuffed imagination
stirred her ice crystal tongue,
sipping the idea of one of those Bud Stamper affairs;
spun fairy floss stockings, deep-rooted Mencken martinis;
smoky humid nights tickled all dewy
with unspoken juniper berry poltergeists;
not the kind of love that kills poetry -
- where everyone is happy and just wants to fuck. No,
this tiffin would release her words
from the bounds of nobility with a garnered dusting
of fine unsweetened innagadadavida translucence;
the kind of words mistaken for revelation;
tympanum to conscience noir
all patchy in discount gloss, hiding behind it
her dirty little past cache intemperance.

barbara w. mcgrory

the kiss

Across this great divide
brown eyes touch
green

Desire dances between us
singing a sweet song
of seduction

Promises and passion reach
a point of no return

The moon hangs high,
this park,
our field of dreams

The zephyr wind undulates
across our skin
igniting sparks of fire!

Desire meets satisfaction

Our souls
meet
in this kiss

and

We sigh
into the
earth

nadine clayton

cinnamon kisses

Deep vanilla-scented kiss,
Inquiring tongue, suffused
With the heady perfume
Of desire: I am light-headed
With sweetness, intoxicated
Near perfect oblivion
And yet, my body so aroused
Each cell vibrates its own unique erotic note
In unison

You! Stealing my breath
My heart, from its deep, protected
Most fortified abode

Oh kiss
Wet, warm, soft
Like catching snow flakes
On my tongue
I close my eyes and tilt my head
Under a moon lit night

Kiss...
A sense of time fading
Running with abandon into the
Wildness of my soul

glenda shaw-garlock

toetry

From the fountain curves of her hips
smooth vanilla legs pour down
to soft french buttercream pastries with
cherry tops in jet black dessert dishes.

She is Page posed, fishnet exposed
hips, whips, and nipple clips;
my leather skin bound to her shapely
body like a corset; six inch heels
pop me like a balloon.

Her feet arch march with strength,
with purpose carrying the weight of battle
Princess Warriors needing rest;
shoe drop dangle, sole breathing.

She buries her toes between me
for the love and warmth of earth;
wet sand hands massage bottoms,
waves of tongue wash over tops;
starfish fingers tickle seashell tipped toes;
legs shaved by the blade of crescent moon.

Veins run through her feet like
vines baring ripe fruit;
toes kissed by morning dew upon
grapes she crushes to make my wine.

Those legs run for miles swaying tall grass
soles crushing bugs, toes painted pink
like a pink rose beneath her clothes.
I have captured her, my fingers move
down her silk spun skin like a spider
finding prey, sinking in.
Her knees are dirty from picking berries;
toe ring jewels chipped from the dance;
silver snake chain, kanji tattoo.

I am the hum to her beat
slave to the chain
Lion at her feet

    frank axworthy

kiss to crying

"Why do you bite my lip, when we kiss?"
I asked her.
She looked me in the eyes, squarely and said
"Sometimes I get so turned on, my animal instincts says bite...
and your lip is the closest thing to my teeth..."
"Then why do you cry after we make love?"
Is it because you're filled with emotion and can't hold it in
or because you're not sure,
 if we'll be doing this again...
And she just stares at me blankly.
Mouth agape,
Saying nothing.

BlackMarket

insatiable night

Rhythms twilight-meld
crashing ocean.

I melody my tongue with your lips
that command, my ache to drift
up your thighs awake
teasing

The aroma
that anticipates pleas
of a silken spread to quake
in core-need

I grip of your carnal demand
of our pleasure-dove in fold
to encapsulate
within the break free

Exhaustion recites sighs that gleam
undertow-flicker
in candlelit black lace cotton

Drenching insatiable
to daybreak moonlight
in fever pitch tight.

courtney ray

maiden grass

Your eyes
buzz about
lazy linger
on my mouth.

Summer heavy lids
suspended
over
meadows,
unhurried rustle
of tumbling
tussling
maiden grass.

Your mouth
a blush of henna
filigree on my neck,
decree of jubilee
whispered in my ear,
to release joy
let it loose
and peal
in the ruffling
and unruffling
of banners
over the width
and length
of my body.

Your tongue,
sweet hum,
m u l l ed wine
bel canto
shadow chords
and bass roots
stir
shaken cantatas
between my thighs,

flesh anointing
for the call.

To move
to your
bidding
rhythm.

anna donovan

there

There
where your muted firth caromed
and hastened it's tempo
disenchantment became a whisper
There
I froze, in the cold lap of disfavor
your common dance so lacking;
accosting, and so in need of my acceding
There
in your unworldly slaver
self-impressed dexterity; prosaic
untoward vellicate style
There
what about my needs
capsheaf ineluctable; arched--
prone to your circumnavigation
There
alleviated to vexation
the emphasis you suggest
brings a threat to my structure
There
seized once more, suspended again
ensnared in rigid animation
engaged now to your cardinal attention
There
please don't stop and make me hate you
There
my urgency needs to be delivered
There
...wait--no--longer...
There
I said
There
godammit

  f
   a
    s
     t
      ~
       i
      ~
g
i
u
m

stop moving for one fucking second
There

      barbara w. mcgrory

head sex

You read my words to lubricate your mind
My contractions are your four-play
Mind fucking is my forte
I spread your ears wide
To accommodate the girth of my tongue
Licking at your synapses
"Show me how you work that brain baby"
I push my love inside
With dead aim I hit your elusive mental G spot
No place to hide tonight you're mine
The pace of my cadence interrupts thought patterns
Neck muscles tense at the pressure building in your head
Subliminal orgasms
Resonate
Lingers long after we have cum
Your mind is a sopping mess of what I've said
And try as you may it can't be wiped clean
It stays
Until the seeds of love grow
Inside your frontal lobe
"No back burner for this man"
I can't wait to get to the rest of you

BlackMarket

the perfect canvas

A single touch with these gentle lips
Emotions evoked from deep within
Fingertips tracing flawed perfection
Sighed shivers, masked guilty pleasures

Shallow breaths begin to quicken
As your eyes flutter to a close
Senses slowly merge together
Let's take our time, pretend there's forever

This is not love cause I am not in love
Though your body makes the perfect canvas
Slightly tainted as most normally are
But this is different, you're more complex

You will notice nothing with eyes sealed shut
Your confusion is overwhelming, slow it down
Let your thoughts gently drift away
Give in to temptation, forget all reason

brenda patricia garza

there is nothing better than sex in the kitchen

There is nothing
better than sex in the kitchen;
with you laid out flat
like a fat cat that's got the cream.
How I dream of that grin
spread as far and wide as my thirty-two and a half inch legs
wrapped around your chest.

When we rest we smoke;
not in bed but wrapped in sheets
and shirts in the garden.
Huddled together for extra warmth
and the heat that greets me
rising from your body;
as an invisible steam
moves me back to places we have just been.

Blowing smoke rings in your face
you race to cup your hands around mine;
so bone fine and pale white.
Light from the window
making long shadows across dewy grass,
until at last you reach
underneath my layers of wrapping.

And so strapping are you;
when you run those working hands
all over my convex curves.
I swerve into your arms
falling fast into the deep pools
of love that turn towards the sun.

I am undone by your lust

So we lay in the flower beds
full of geraniums and daisies;

crazy with a passion that lifts
and dips as the tides of time.
I am mine and yours
gorged in greedy hunger and need;
freed from all that
which lingered before.

samantha ledger

this ancient song

made new.

your hands

make birdshadows

beat against a wall

our pavilion

its' silks and streamers

flutter in the chill

breeze of after - noon

await the still

- pause -

the space between

the indrawn breath of day

the slow sigh of night

a moment in time
a moment away
a moment.

.now.

your hands

make birdshadows

beat against a wall

    bruce dorlova

oh yes

Bush baby, cabbage patch, earth deep salty sea smell.
Lacy large against dart daring loined tongue.
Your hips roll, your mons' curve,
your breasts soften to clouds hovering

and I ride through your valleys multiplied like an army.
My elephants, my stallions, my wounds, my sad failures
all given the gift, the gift of your giving

and I hide by your shoulder of boat bones and sand sweep
as we kiss cling decided by lifetimes of longing.
Shower bathing your sea valve with the spit wish of fathers.

And I die like a flower, like a slow motion cowboy
and you quiver like the arrow, like the earth when it buckles
and this is a memory I hold to my heart,
my heart needs its warming.

ross hamilton hill

felt

Bitter skin
gave way to the sweetest skin,
her thighs and,
rapid suffocation.

"It ain't gonna' eat itself, sunshine."

Two lane roads put you
four feet from death every time you pass
yet, petty thoughts don't matter when...

Bitter skin gives way to the
sweetest skin with,
rapid suffocation
between her thighs.

BlackMarket

augury

*To him she sang a hex of
her pit-fractured pleasure.*

Six times about the bearing tree,
bite and bark enfolded;
one lisping charm curled
unforgiving about her throat.

Six times a curse laid waste
to supple flesh tainted
with scent of his panting;
no mercy in casual seeding.

Six times she bore him off
as crackled life fell away;
a whipped and wedded wraith,
she banshee-rode his disdain.

*Deftly she shelled his meat
and consumed him entire.*

dale winslow

foreplay

A lush sweetness, humidity and ardor
Flutters over the looming horizon.
In a distance, our room,
Melodies peek in high tones
And resistively playful pleasure moans.

You were calling, taunting me.
Seducing me with you cadent tongue,
Your torched hairs of lilacs
And stretched marine sheets with a scent of lavender.

Your eyes floating buoys and maritime guides,
Setting the bait for your desires to keep.
You were calling, chanting longings
And asking, begging your cravings to submerge.

You called.

Now, that I'm steering rhythms atop of you,
Your tail caught in my net,
There's no more night harmonics
Calm seas; It is now and you're mine.

Let's see what tune you'll compose,
Under the deluge of my wafting passion.

josé e. del rosario

NeoPoiesis
a new way of making

in ancient Greece, poiesis referred to the process of making
creation – production – organization – formation – causation
a process that can be physical and spiritual
biological and intellectual
artistic and technological
material and teleological
efficient and formal
a means of modifying the environment
and a method of organizing the self
the making of art and music and poetry
the fashioning of memory and history and philosophy
the construction of perception and expression and reality

NeoPoiesis Press
reflecting the creative drive and spirit
of the new electronic media environment

www.ingramcontent.com/pod-product-compliance
Lightning Source LLC
Chambersburg PA
CBHW072201100426
42738CB00011BA/2491